REIMAGINING JONAH

A Flight to Freedom

DOUG WHEELER

For my brother, Dick, who left us on December 26, 2016, who I imagine alongside Ronnie Van Zant, barefoot and smiling, rocking into the forever.

For my father, Port, who courageously revealed his love for me in his last days. I now understand the pain hidden in his silence.

And for my mother, Patricia, who confidently delivered me into two worlds, the physical and the spiritual. I will forever be grateful. Her love for God was real.

CONTENTS

Introduction xi

Ruminating 1

Running 7

Sinking 13

Settling 21

Rising 29

Differentiating 35

Disrupting 43

Disintegrating 51

Empowering 59

Conclusion 69

Grant me the grace to reclaim these depths
to uncover this treasure
to liberate these longings
and in being set free in my own spirit
to act for the well-being of the world.

— J. Phillip Newell, Celtic Benediction*

Introduction

My journey with Jonah began in 2016, when I was invited by a good friend to speak at his church. I chose the famed Jonah story for my sermon, more from a practical need for palatable scripture than any special liking for it. I approached the story with low-grade interest and a basic knowledge of its familiar reductions: a prophet gone rogue, miraculously saved by a whale, who (finally) relented to a relentless God. Simple takeaways, right? Yet, as a man in the second half of life, as a husband and father, as one having endured agonizing loss, I read Jonah through new eyes. I was moved, I was hooked, and I enthusiastically titled my sermon, "Jonah as Guide." Thus, the seeds of this book were sown.

What awoke in me was a relentless empathy for Jonah. I imagined our interior worlds as mutually befriended. We knew each other. I sensed Jonah had a degree of social phobia, as I do. His family wounds mirrored my own. And through that kindredness, it became clear to me: Jonah needed defending. Is it possible his voice had been hijacked by dogma, manipulated as praise and repentance rather than the legitimate and necessary cries of protest and self-actualization? Seeing Jonah as a person-before-prophet piqued my fascination with the psychodynamics (mental and emotional forces) that shaped his selfhood. What were his unique contexts? Who was he? Why did no one care? As a psychotherapist, I had to look deeper.

The prevailing caricature of Jonah is one of pitiful cowardice and narcissism, an archetypal loser in need of divine correction. Because the story's interpretation has been so biased toward the need for blind obedience, both Jonah and his God have been in perpetual lockdown, with little opportunity for new expressions. Theologians and laity alike have portrayed Jonah as the defiant prophet who ran, while failing to understand he was fleeing far more than the voice of his God. I wanted to present a dimension of the story missed, interpreting Jonah's running as a method of discovering self *through* disobedience.

In Professor Jack M. Sasson's Jonah: A New Translation, he presents God's discernment of Jonah's mood as dejected rather than angry, a rare suggestion of empathy toward the prophet. This alone affirmed my belief that Jonah was genuinely suffering from a lifetime of cultural and familial adversity and launched me headfirst into a strange, imaginary dialogue with the prophet that teetered between prose and narrative. This book is a mosaic of ideas, a kind of character study, a confluence of psychoanalysis and active imagination that personalizes this mythic tale. There is a fair bit of myself woven into these interpretations as I processed grief and rebirth alongside Jonah in real time. Ultimately, he became an illusory client, friend, and confidant.

I do not claim to be an academic or forensic authority here. I am not a biblical scholar, nor am I formally credentialed in linguistics, theology, or other similar disciplines. I am a practicing therapist of thirty-five years with deep interest in psychotherapy, psychodrama, and spiritual formation. After decades of tepid religiosity and a recent season of agnostic meditation, this book flowed from me in a way that felt like detox and reclamation bundled together, a poetic *reimagining* of a story I thought I knew but had only been *told* I knew. So, thank you, reader, for embarking here. Whatever need or curiosity brought you, may it be met.

I'D BE REMISS if I did not mention the muse that took my hand in this process. Music became the backdrop to countless hours of typing, and one night, a particular song brought Jonah as close as my own breath. From there, I began to curate a playlist that energized me and spoke to the themes at play. I have placed a lyric from each of those songs at the head of each chapter to impress upon you their importance. I highly recommend listening to them as you move through *Reimagining Jonah*.

Ruminating

I've been boxed-in in the lowlands, in the canyons that think

I've been pushed to the brink of the precipice and dared not to blink

I've been confounded in the whirlwind of what-ifs and dreams

I've been burned by the turning of the wind back upon my own flames

Knock the scales from my eyes

Knock the words from my lungs

I want to cry out

It's on the tip of my tongue

— **Excerpt from** *Tip of My Tongue* **by Mark Heard**

Jonah,

I can see your pain on the page, as if oozing onto my fingers. I can feel it as I read, your looming anxiety doing its insidious work. As a child, you were too young to understand its origin, too inexperienced to hold off its attacks. Its pull toward a living hell was never-ending. Your suffering had grown from an ancestral shadow tainting the family bloodline. The day your father raged when he tore his skin on a bramble bush revealed hidden things. It took only moments for him to return to his stoicism. He seemed dangerous to ever cross, so you learned to steer clear of him.

At times, even your dear mother would break, like the day she lunged at a group of boys bludgeoning a lamb caught in a prickly thicket, threatening them with violence. As they tore off, she gently picked up the small, terrified creature and whispered words of comfort as she observed its wounds. Her fierce love also soothed a deep and anonymous wound inside you. Her danger was born from compassion, a safer fire.

At birth, your father was given the name *Truth* and singled out as a prophet by your grandfather and the men of his tribe. He played the role well, never voicing doubt, never questioning the beliefs of the forefathers. God was to be worshiped as the supreme controller of all life — a purveyor of judgment and consequence. You dreamt of a different God, one who was freer, kinder, and merciful toward all people. The older you grew, the lesser was your drive to follow the unyielding God of your father, an entity known for doling out violence. A secret desire to escape your trappings pulsated through you, causing such conflict with your compliant self. You longed for a space to be free of being the obedient son.

Your father saw his strength and the future of his faith in you. You were born to carry his legacy, a responsibility you never asked for and increasingly (but secretly) rejected. Your thoughts of escape often kept you up at night, along with the fear your father would somehow find you out. Did your mother lay awake, wrestling with similar conflicts?

You were born into privilege, into a family rich with resources, which set you apart. I imagine the other kids your age held a grudge against you for it or at the very least envied you. They understood all too well that you held a higher station than them, that you would be handed the position of prophet. They never imagined you would gladly trade places with any one of them. You'd dreamt of their life, free from the constant fear of disapproval. You felt like a captive within the high-walled prison of familial expectation.

You were prepped early on to hear a call from God. You had secretly hoped the call would encourage freedom, to loosen the chains of obedience. But instead, it was a call for violence against a neighboring city, for full-on destruction to be enacted by your voice:

"SET OUT FOR NINEVEH, THAT LARGE CITY, AND DECLARE DOOM UPON IT; THE WICKEDNESS OF ITS CITIZENS IS OBVIOUS TO ME."[1]

Again, the inner conflict raged. The "obedient son" inside you wanted to answer the call, to fulfill your father's wish, but you couldn't imagine doing it. A stinging shame swelled at the possibility of failing your father, accompanied by guilt for desiring to run. Could there be another God other than your father's? As your anxiety intensified, you remembered a song your mother and grandmother had sung countless times to you and your siblings. The song's chorus, "It will be quiet when peace returns" had often quelled a troubled moment.

As you wrestled with the command, you wondered if God was simply a figment of your community's imagination, a propaganda passed down by the forefathers to secure allegiance and garnish a way of life superior to outsiders. As you began to differentiate your own voice which challenged the community's dogma, it began to sharply whisper, "Escape!" But where would you go, and how in the world would you get there? Running away felt like a betrayal of family, of *self* even, and a feat beyond your ability.

Permission would never come from your father, your mother, or your teachers, but your instinct told you clearly, there was freedom and grace in a world beyond. An inner voice was gaining momentum and one day it penetrated your resistance, forming a living image in your mind of making a break for it.

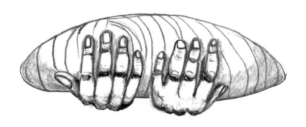

Running

Out in the parking lot

The ground is beating hot

There are no raindrops on my shoes

I got no license plate

I come from out-of-state

A town where children sing the blues

Guess, all my running was worth the chance

And now I'm glad because

I've flown this acid world

Yes, I've flown this acid world

I see the chimney smoke

Follow the family folk

All covered up in sheets of red

A sad dalmatian waits against the western gate

He tries to steal my piece of bread

Guess, I'll go hungry for the night again

— **Excerpt from** *Flown This Acid World* **by Peter Himmelman**

Jonah,

I can imagine how difficult it was to trust yourself to flee, to leave behind the only life you'd ever known. How could this be the right thing to do when it conjured up so much fear? When it was in direct opposition to all you'd been taught? It felt impulsive, childish even; oppositional inner voices pronounced disgust for your betrayal. Still, you ran. You angrily kicked up the dust in defiance of your father's immovable beliefs, forced upon you from birth. You ran to escape the confusion and hurt which had warred inside you. I'm sure you were tempted to stop, turn around, and return home to the familiar norms, to sanctuary, but a warrior-energy pushed you forward.

Your father did all he could to mold you into his image. His psychological and emotional pain colored his aspirations for you. Fathers often do this to their sons, many times unknowingly. When you were a young boy, your mother and grandmother had tried to compensate for your father's hard ways, but his demeanor continued to wound you, season after season. You didn't have the tools to protect yourself, as it's a father's job to equip his son with the necessary armor for battle. He was supposed to be your advocate, not your adversary. You were utterly disheartened.

Despite all this heartache, you loved your family. This made fleeing all the harder; however, the pressure had become too great. You thought about the shame your unannounced departure would bring upon them. Your siblings would ridicule you for leaving, especially your brothers. They were always at odds with your favored position, full of jealousy and resentment. They would never understand why you, the firstborn, the chosen, would gladly sacrifice your prophet status. You could almost hear their gnashing of teeth, while silently strategizing how they might vie for the now vacant role of prophethood. All the while, your sisters would say nightly prayers for your protection and cry themselves to sleep, along with your mother and grandmother.

All you wanted was to be seen for who you were. Becoming a prophet of violence was not native to your disposition; talk of retribution, of enemies of the *Lord God* and His people, of warring against neighboring "outsiders," had grown ugly. Your father warned you of these enemies of God. Your mother told you your curiosity would prove hazardous. Somehow you knew they were wrong, but you had no evidence to challenge their fiery admonitions and zealous fortitude.

As the sun crept down, you reached the border of your land and stopped at the river's edge to soak your tired feet. You nodded off but soon woke to see a figure down river, an old man fishing along a rocky section of the riverbank. His clothes were tattered but otherwise no different from those of your people. He looked up at you, curly white hair peeking out from beneath the strange cap on his head. At first, you were frightened, recalling all the horrors you'd been told. Afterall, here was one of those "others." But he smiled and gestured for you to come near, speaking a strange tongue.

You responded in your own speech, but his face confirmed the language barrier. He wordlessly offered you a bit of bread from his basket, and the two of you sat together into the early evening. He built a fire and cooked up the day's catch. You slept like a baby through the night and, in the morning, thanked him with a firm embrace. As you walked away, you tucked that experience into your heart like a secret treasure. If those on the "outside" could be this warm and brotherly, could the harsh characterizations of your tribe's God be equally unfounded?

Your people praised an exacting God ready and willing to punish, and you fixated on what He would now do to you in your disobedience. The religious teachings etched into your psyche rose with force. You stopped on the hillside to take a breath, shaking your head to somehow loosen the tangled web inside. If God knows all and was at times as loving as your teachers extolled, doesn't He understand your desperate need to escape? To spare the souls of Nineveh by foregoing judgment? Drifting to the side of the path, you sat under a tree until your breathing calmed. You closed your eyes and were reminded why you left: to spare *yourself*. The voices of condemnation quieted, and you rested.

Your mind turned to the hunts with the men of your tribe. You weren't particularly strong or gifted with a weapon, but you were fast, faster than all the other boys. And you had a natural gift for tracking. You would take the lead, find the prey, and witness the takedown. You understood the need for food, but you were repulsed to watch the adult men celebrate the kill. You repeatedly fantasized about the prey escaping, imagining the men feeling like failures. Sometimes you'd imagine that you were the prey, too wily, quick, and cunning to be caught. You'd heckle them as you laughed your way back into the thicket. With these thoughts, you fell asleep, soothed on the inside, guarded by the gathering darkness of blue hour.

As morning broke, you pressed forward into no man's land. At times, you cried uncontrollably as your mummified heart had broken open. As your shadow appeared before you on the path, you saw it as God's angry face. His voice rose, stern and fiery, hell-bent on turning you back.

You literally vomited your breakfast when reciting His commandment to help destroy Nineveh. Something deep inside you yearned for a different God, a gentler presence than the one you were trying to outrun. Perhaps it was magical thinking, but even so, it gave you a modicum of relief. Travailing the steep hill, you saw a coastline for the first time.

Sinking

But my dreams, they aren't as empty

As my conscience seems to be

I have hours, only lonely

My love is vengeance that's never free

When my fist clenches, crack it open

Before I use it and lose my cool

When I smile, tell me some bad news

Before I laugh and act like a fool

And if I swallow anything evil

Put your finger down my throat

And if I shiver, please give me a blanket

Keep me warm, let me wear your coat

No one knows what it's like

To be the bad man, to be the sad man

Behind blue eyes

— **Excerpt from** *Behind Blue Eyes* **by Peter Townshend**

Jonah,

You walked into Jaffa, a port swarming with "others." You marveled as you made your way through the dense market, their ways and customs so foreign to you. "Pagan" was the verbiage used by your people, a scornful term applied to those non-chosen ones who didn't follow the Hebrew God. You were supposed to be afraid and on guard, but you felt oddly drawn to them. You watched the elderly engage in their trades as children carelessly ran about. Their laughter awoke an empty feeling that began to swallow you. Yet, as you approached the docks, this strange ache became excitement.

A cargo ship crept up to the dock where you stood. It felt like it had landed just for you. The ship's lively crew put you on pause; you weren't used to such rowdiness. But stronger than intimidation was an appetite for adventure, so you contemplated buying passage. You flashed the money you'd stolen from your father's satchel, a week's wage at sea. You named Tarshish as your destination, having heard it was welcoming to strangers, and waited anxiously for the captain's reply. "Come aboard," he'd grunted.

The crew took notice of you quickly, eyeing your linen clothes and the specific shade of your skin. Theirs too was dark-toned, but from toiling under the hot sun, not from being born of chosen lineage. They remained perplexed. This ship carried mercantile goods, weapons, and fish, not passengers. Three sailors cornered you asking, "Why are you traveling alone? What business have you in Tarshish?" Your answers didn't satisfy their suspicions, but despite their callousness, you felt oddly strong in their presence.

You sat cross-legged in a barren corner below deck, while the crew loaded the ship and prepared to set sail. As you laid your head on a small bag of clothes taken from home, the familiar smells of it flooded your body with anxiety, causing you to pant for air. Just days before, you'd been commanded by the Almighty to be a mouthpiece of holy retribution toward a people you knew very little about, not unlike this ship's crew. What would they do to you if they found out your history? Your story?

In time, you fell asleep and descended into a dream. Sitting before a night fire at the center of a dry lakebed, with stars overhead, you opened your eyes. Sitting beside you was Ahmose, the daughter of a poor farmer back home. Her bright eyes framed by coal-black hair, wild and uncombed, made you feel alive. You both talked for hours, falling in love for the first time. After saying goodnight, you snuck back home to find your parents brooding at the table. Glaring at you, your father asked where you'd been; you told them the truth. He was livid. You had shamed his good name, along with your entire family. Your mother said nothing as your father voiced his disgust. You stared into his fiery eyes and promised to never again see Ahmose. You pleaded with them to forgive your foolishness and swore an oath to marry one of their choosing.

You woke up gasping for air, as the dream revealed a buried truth in your unconscious. You still loved Ahmose and wanted to be with her. Believing this would never happen, you wanted to be dead, right then and there. You felt the heat of rage inside you, more like your father's than you'd ever want to admit. Next came intense hatred, not of him or your God, but of yourself. It was all the same hatred, the same rage, permeating everything, burying you deep. And all of this compounded your lifelong struggle with unnamed suicidality.

Flooded with dread, you landed at the bottom of the lowest of lows, completely void of light. Hesitantly standing, you were immediately thrown back on your ass. The ship was in a God-sized storm. An angry God! Running to the top deck, you found the crew fighting a wall of blinding rain, praying to their own gods for deliverance. Amidst the chaos, a strange calm fell over you. It was no doubt the calm of that ideation, that death-wanting, that numbness. So, you returned to the belly of the ship and fell back to sleep, inexplicably, hoping for a reunion with Ahmose in the quiet of the past. But within minutes, you were shook awake by the captain, urging you to appeal to whomever you worshipped for their survival in the tempest.

As the storm raged, the sailors cast lots to identify who was at fault. It predictably fell on you, Jonah. A flurry of questions arose about your past, your people, and your motives for travel. They wanted the truth. You spoke of being a Hebrew and about the God of your people. You spoke of the call and of running. You called yourself a prophet. So, these brawny sailors fell at your feet and pleaded with you to make things right. This triggered a crippling shame inside you. You offered your own plea, one that secretly fulfilled your desire: "Cast me into the sea."

The sailors were reluctant, fearing this fierce Hebrew God they'd heard tell of. Afterall, you belonged to this God, and He was jealous of His belongings. But the deal was struck. They threw you overboard like a limp fish, and as you hit the cold water, the oxygen in your lungs turned to ice.

A tall wave held you high enough to see the sailors peering at you, forming a portrait of trepidation, contempt, empathy, relief, and even love. It was as if your insides were projected onto their faces, ushering you into some unknown *presence.* Your mind traveled at light speed with scenes of loved ones, landscapes, wild things in the air and on foot, night skies, ceremonies of life and death, tribal hunts, extended feasts, and so much more. As you sank, you prayed to die quickly and live miraculously, a prayer no one had ever taught you. You wondered, "Where did this strange prayer come from, and what did it mean?"

You asked the God of your parents if you'd die before you hit bottom. Why were you praying again? Did you still believe in their God? You had wanted to run far away and never think of God again, to be relieved of the prophet-noose tied around your neck. And what of your father and all his preaching about integrity, obedience, and righteousness? All those qualities that constitute a pious life. Wasn't he a hypocrite for never sharing any difficulties from his childhood? Had he too rebelled against God or at least contemplated it but somehow found his way back into the sacred fold? Why did you still love him, a father so closed off from his own son? Why were you thinking of this in your last moments? So many questions would not be answered.

Jonah, your destiny was vastly different from your father's, as you would die alone, memorialized by your people as a cowardly dissenter. Your story would now be canonized as a tale of great warning for those who disobey God's voice. You had sealed your own fate.

You just wanted to die quickly, Jonah. But what about the prayer to "live miraculously?"

Settling

I wish I didn't rely

On that robot voice to be my guide

But I

Always do

So I'll follow her blue dot all over the map

Try to pay attention but

I'm never quite sure

Where I'm at

So you can find me where I'm lost

You can find me where I'm lost

I just can't pretend

That this doesn't happen a lot

So you can find me

Where I said I'm not

Never had a surprise party

But I've had a search party

Never had a surprise party

But I've had a search party

— **Excerpt from** *Lost* **by Sienna Meadow**

Jonah,

The sailors performed a ceremony of penance moments after you fell into the sea. This ritual was meant to concretize their regret for their wrongdoing and to possibly, strangely, engage their love for *you*, the victim. It's sad that all of this was lost on you, as you were destined to die alone at sea's bottom, with no hope of ever receiving a visit to your watery gravesite. Your harsh ending appears commensurate with your failed attempt to escape your prophetic calling, to escape your predestined responsibilities.

You'd tried for years to be what you were supposed to be, what you were apparently born for, who your father (and his father) had groomed you to become, and what your mother (and her mother) oddly needed you to be. Mother and grandmother's roles were complicated, as they both loved you genuinely. As women, they were confined to the proverbial prisons of their own; how could they hope to spring you from yours? But their fierce love, along with the hope of Ahmose's love, had kept a chamber of your heart warm and tender, as warm and tender as the flesh that had suddenly enveloped you and scooped you up in the depths.

On my Sunday school wall hung a small painting of you, Jonah. More precisely, a caricature of you. It depicted an emaciated man with a scruffy beard, perched alone, looking forlorn. Suffice to say, he was "down in the mouth." Beside him, an oil lamp rested atop a thin-legged table, expressing a dim light into a vacuous cavern. Etched on the frame of this painting were the words, "Jonah Inside the Whale." The image itself, so cartoonish in nature, made me question what my eyes saw. A human being swallowed by a creature of the sea, appearing unscathed and living comfortably?

I find the literality of this part of your story unimportant. Whether by historical account or profound metaphor, you were indeed swallowed, Jonah. I've named the sea creature in question "She-Fish." One of many translations of the Hebrew word used in the story is of a feminine per-suasion. This promotes a shift in interpretation for what took place in Her belly, something essential for true transformation. I imagine Her impulse was to bathe you in Her salty amniotic fluids, those carried by mammalian mothers for birthing purposes. As an Islamic friend of mine once said, "Jonah had to go back inside the womb and grow again."

You were twenty-four hours into your womb-time, but conscious time wasn't important as you weren't in command. You'd been forced into total darkness, where internal shadows loomed large and the content buried deep within bubbled up. Your serious attention was called upon. The lov-ing timbre of the She-Fish's voice was calling forth your buried pain into conscious view. You wept, and wept, and wept, and then you unleashed a litany of speech, being painfully and outwardly honest for the first time. It took great courage for you to go there, even in talking to the solitary walls of Her fleshy belly. A waft of saltwater in your nostrils triggered the ques-tion, "What is this vessel I'm being held in?"

Screaming out loud opened a portal in you. You fearlessly addressed your father regarding all the junk he'd displaced onto you. His unresolved pain had so burdened you, his firstborn. Then you turned to your mother, asking her why she didn't intervene, why she hadn't advocated for you? You tried to imagine your father being remorseful, and your mother running to hug you. This was not fantasy-thinking but was representative of your hunger for familial safety and restitution. You softened and fell still for a moment. What returned was the timeless hurt and need for more outcry.

Protest speech again leapt out of you and the tears returned . . . years of tears. Suddenly a fractal of light appeared through a generous slit within arm's reach. You touched the rim of the opening and an energy flowed upward to your lips. The protest ceased. You intuited this light was streaming through the very throat that had swallowed you, and you *knew* beyond doubt you'd been saved by a benevolent thing. Resting in place, you caught a soothing breath, as the air was both lighter and brighter. The slow, steady movement of the She-Fish had wooed you into a peace you'd never known. A safe silence filled you with hope and made you want to live. Eclipsed by this loving presence, your death wish sunk to an unknown bottom. No longer did you hear your father's gravelly voice droning on with inconsolable demands. You could now hear crystal clear your *own* voice harmonizing with the She-Fish's sweet, soothing breath, which whispered your name repeatedly, "Jonah, Jonah, Jonah . . ."

What was She trying to communicate to you? Was She asking you to do something, something special? Were you to fully trust the She-Fish? With all these unknowns, you listened to your gut's clear voice, "Draw close and listen as She is wholeheartedly trustworthy."

Within moments, you heard the She-Fish say, "Feel my love; accept my strength. Heal." As you processed the offer, She spoke again, "I accept everything about you, and I will teach you how to do this for yourself." A new voice entered your head, this time your own, saying, "Turn toward yourself with love. Now turn."

I, too, had a transformative spiritual experience. One December night, forty-four years ago, I called upon Jesus Christ to rescue me from unbearable inner pain. I've spent many hours since that winter night, asking, "*Who* repaired me and *what* exactly got repaired?" What I know is that my *Self*, the truest essence of *Me*, had become inoperable due to trauma at a very vulnerable age. The language spoken for me of being "born again" made perfect sense, as something "dead" had been restored. Sadly, I quickly succumbed to others' expectations about my rebirth that postponed my need of doing the psychoanalytic work. I'm still doing that work today.

Jonah, some part of you wanted out, to feel your waterlogged skin dry in the hot sun and to try again to live on your own two feet. Another part of you wanted to stay inside, to cling to this benevolent gestation, as you'd experienced a powerful dose of self-esteem. You couldn't comprehend the lasting impact of your conversion experience, and therefore, weren't sure of its value in the other world, the outside world, the world governed by men.

But you knew your fate was not within your grasp, as you hadn't initiated the grand rescue, nor could you influence the great She-Fish's decision to release or keep you. A young part of you quickly became aroused with protective energy, and anxiety saturated your whole body. Accusing voices showed up from God knows where? Perhaps God himself? More of your oppressors will need to be confronted, but that work is for another time.

Your She-Fish, without a hint of hesitation, called you back to a relaxed body, and you rested in place.

Rising

Behind the wardrobe there lies a better life

Burn all your old clothes start again make yourself something new

And the bed you've made no you need not sleep in it

Throw back the covers and make all of your dreams come true

Rebuild your life rebuild your home rethink your values

Rethink yourself right through

I have declared myself unsafe

I have declared myself unsafe

Unsound, unknown, unwanted, unnecessary

I've been condemned

I'm unsafe

— **Excerpt from** *Unsafe Building* **by Michael Peters and Edward MacDonald**

Jonah,

You landed headfirst onto the shore, the result of the She-Fish's divine regurgitation. She serenely glided away in the background, having Her own life to live, Her own quests, Her own world to explore.

Early scribes used a native word (as a literary device) to signify a holy pause immediately after Jonah's return to dry ground and before God's renewed call to go to Nineveh. What took place in this in-between, splitting two such moments of lasting significance?

I can only imagine how wobbly you were as you attempted to stand, with a thousand-and-some thoughts bouncing like wild jackrabbits in your head. A waft of worldly smells hits your nostrils, and you instinctively breathed deep, finding a warmth in the center of your chest. The She-Fish's love had crossed the blood–brain barrier, miraculously seeping into your consciousness.

Looking outward into the dry desert, you asked, "What now?" While remaining in place, you felt an energy pulling you downward, as if you were to enter a deeper interior chamber unknown to you. You automatically held your breath, sensing that something beyond your control was about to happen, something big.

An image appeared, vibrating with multi-dimensional colors. It was a whole fig, ripe for tasting. It hovered before you, pulsating with energy, emanating heat waves akin to the desert sun. You were tempted to grasp it, but it wouldn't allow you to. The swollen fig began to split down the middle slowly and sensually, and soon, two bite-sized pieces fell at your feet. As you bent down, each piece asked in its own voice, "Jonah, are you sure you want to taste me?" You closed your eyes and asked, "Am I hallucinating? Is this a weird vision from above? Have I gone crazy from my time in the She-Fish's belly?" Each piece of fig seemed oddly significant to your future.

With some hesitation, you bit into one of the pieces of fig and immediately moaned from its sweetness, whispering, "Damn, that's good." You bit the other piece and quickly puckered, gasping from both its bitter taste and foul odor. You quickly spat it out and felt a wave of rage atop a deeper layer of disgust. This entire experience rendered you overwhelmed, psychologically flooded. It felt like certain parts of you were fighting recklessly for dominance, whereas other parts were retreating in fear. It was an interior battleground.

The voices of your village pummeled your thoughts, words of violence and conquest set to tribal songs, sung repeatedly, declaring war on the "others." Large animal-skinned drums carried the lyrics, beating ferociously, harkening a forthcoming drama. With your mind's eye, you could see yourself standing amongst dense layers of human carnage, half-burnt corpses stacked like firewood: mothers, fathers, grandmothers, grandfathers, and children of all ages. The rotted piece of fig swelled, and you vomited. Staring at the stained sand underfoot, you recognized the grotesque hatred in these memories.

Your mind turned to the sweet piece of fig, luscious and succulent to your lips. You inquired, "What value do you hold?" This time, you didn't hear a voice other than your own, and you trusted your voice fully for the first time. Soon, a pictorial scene emerged, chock-full of high-resolution colors, in direct opposition to the field of carnage earlier. The benevolent, generous scenery affirmed the value of all human life. You felt the stabilizing presence of faith, hope, and love, with love being the supreme winner. You broke out in wild laughter and cried tears of joy.

As you began to walk inland, thoughts of the fig consumed your every step. "Why did the fig appear as a unified whole, then split into two identically sized pieces? How could one be utterly rotten and the other so sweetly ripe, having come from the same fruit?" Your eyes had *seen* a dividing line between the fig pieces, disallowing any mixing of disparate materials. One co-ed tribal ritual came to mind, where light and laughter were called upon through fire and dance. This ritual represented the ripe piece of fig! You thought, "*Choice* is within everyone's grasp, to honor *all* life as sacred." You prayed your tribe would never again sing songs of war. The She-Fish returned to your mind. You still felt Her loving embrace, Her call to calm, Her wild deliverance. She had cradled you so delicately.

You peered at the horizon line and wondered what awaited you in the vast lands ahead.

Differentiating

And the building was on fire

When I saw you step out

Afraid of your ghosts, and highly in doubt

When you knew along

Not even your cloud

Would ever withstand the song from your mouth

So they took all your scripts

And the rain from your eyes

They're cashing it in for the next passing ride

To some other city you made up in your mind

They missed when you died

So they're hitting rewind

What good is living if you can't write your ending?

You're always in doubt of the truths you're defending

— **Excerpt from** *The Last Great Washington State* **by Damien Jurado**

Jonah,

In his masterpiece poem, "The Everlasting Gospel," nineteenth-century poet William Blake spoke of seeing not with but through one's eye. This form of seeing penetrates a depth which lies beyond what's obvious, bringing into sharp focus distinctions that up to that point have remained opaque. The concept of differentiation, defined as the ability to recognize what makes someone or something different, is the result of the seeing, Blake promotes.

When related to human development, differentiating promotes individuation, which is best understood to be the process of forming a stable personality. If a person can differentiate/individuate, they will gain a clearer sense of who they are, separate from their parents and others around them.

A profound differentiation happened to you as you walked alone into the wayward borderlands. You were Renamed; no longer were you "Jonah, son of Amittay," but simply, uniquely, undeniably "Jonah." This renaming stoked a fiery energy in your consciousness, and you felt authentically alive for the first time ever. It was as if something surgical had taken place inside your gut, cutting away the diseased parts from your past, allowing your truest nature to begin to rule. Speaking of "ruling," you were too often surrounded by men of dominance, practicing games of power and control. Your inner chaos has come from the assailing outer chaos they created.

You could now enter your own world and own the damage caused, freeing your enshrouded heart from guilt and shame. You had the power necessary to *heal the wound*, forming a welcoming space inside you, where all the disparate parts of your personality could show themselves. Tread lightly, Jonah, as the pain of a burdened childhood can randomly grab you by the ankles. When it happens, go inward and seek out the part or parts that have been agitated. Move toward them with a welcoming tone.

A hard truth is that the God of your father must die unto you, Jonah. You will falter in the pursuit of that freedom, as the very word "God" elicits such fear. Being taught to behave submissively was a tool used to guarantee submission, to tamp down the need to rise and challenge the practitioners of fear. Ascribing ill motives to your tribal elders (including Amittay) will not loosen the grip they've insured but will, in fact, keep you a prisoner in their world. As I urged earlier, "More of your oppressors will need to be confronted, but that work is for another time." Right now, trust your new identity as it holds the key to the freedom you've yearned for.

There you went, frolicking down the hillside path, as the soles of your feet began to pulsate with raw energy! Scenes of ceremonial dances you used to perform flood your memory. Sadly, Amittay never joined in those holy dances, but that painful wrinkle can't stop your feet from the wildness now. Making a sharp turn too quickly, you gracefully tumbled to your knees and finally came to rest under a lone shade tree. You leaned forward to catch a breath and inadvertently tasted the beads of sweat from your upper lip, triggering two distinct sensations bound as one: the cold seawater seeping into your mouth while sinking to the sea's bottom and the She-Fish's smooth lips pressing against your salt-soaked skin as She swallowed you whole. A grand rescue. A resurrection.

You rested your head on a pillow of moist leaves and fell fast asleep as nothing more or less than "Jonah."

Later, waking, you slowly crawled out from the provisional shelter. Rising from the noonday nap required your eyes to readjust and the brain to refire. Standing upright felt different, like you were both taller and thicker, more put together. A bizarre feeling came over your body and you imagined sprouting wings, effortlessly. You peeked under each armpit, as if the wings were going to appear. In your ears echoed Amittay's mother telling you years ago your given name meant Dove. You imagined flying high into the sky above, bright in color and free of burden, producing a sense of invincibility. Internally, you lifted off and soared high, dangerously high!

This inflation was essential, as the ego must expand (find its wings, if you will) for stability and progress during this critical stage of individuation. We will die on the inside if we don't have natural inflations. All evolutionary "essentials" in identity-building have a natural downturn known as deflation, an event or series of events that counterbalance inflation. But don't despair, Jonah. These experiences are provisional to deliver one's feet back to earth, to ground one in the humble experience of life lived on life's terms. Being human is much more about "walking on the ground" than it is about "flying in the sky." If wings for you are genuine inflation, count on deflation to arrive for a healthy equilibrium meant for your good. A landing.

In the time since you plopped out of the She-Fish's mouth, your ability to comfortably stand, walk, and run had fully returned. About a hundred feet beyond the shade tree, the Command of God suddenly shook the sky above and the ground beneath you, repeating the same message as before:

"SET OUT FOR NINEVEH, THAT LARGE CITY, AND REPORT TO IT THE MESSAGE I TELL YOU."[2]

The magnitude and force of God's demand rattled the cage which once again ensnared you. You swiftly *obeyed*, with no push back, no questioning, no fight, *only* compliance. It was a reflex, a reversion. It was fear. I feel disheartened by your decision to walk to Nineveh with the very feet used for running from Amittay's shadow. You see, Jonah, this *yes* was a relapse, a regression in your growth, an unnecessary detour from advancing your cause. I've seen the price you've paid for your painful departure, your *running*, and I count you a hero for it, a spiritual guide to be trusted. You've *lived* your life, not someone else's, and you have allowed *us* to see *you* live it vulnerably.

You were then hell-bent to go to Nineveh, as in your heart, you'd returned to your familial *home* where father rules the roost. I hold anxiety about the uncertainty of both our futures, so I understand your felt need to grab for *certainty*, something incredibly familiar, even if the return ultimately were to take your life. This reminds me of your desire to die, your suicidality that biblical scholars, laymen, and the very Bible itself appear blind to.

The dominant opinion among Bible believers is that you've returned to your holy senses, to that *son* in you that obeys his father and elders alike, to reestablishing yourself as God's chosen prophet. My ears ring with those cheering you on to deliver God's threat of divine punishment for the unrighteousness practiced in Nineveh. You've been recalled into doing God's bidding, and according to popular religious opinion, you're all the better for it.

Ironically, your future well-being was no match for what the Lord of your people needed. How could it compare to the zealots? But what did you get out of the deal? The loser's card. You're the prophet popularized by failure, an embodiment of delegitimization. A genuine sham. Sadly, your decision to comply has been memorialized and fallen prey to the *magical thinking* of the *religious type*. We, who've been on the inside, know well the Christian teaching explicitly stating that God offers "special protection to and covering for those who obey."

Jonah, your earlier differentiation from your father's world, heard as an inner voice calling your birth name, was not a dream, delusion, or ego inflation. It *happened* and you *knew* it! What you might not have known is that your *Renaming* had been written and the ink dried. The whole world can *see* your individuation in motion, that is, if they want to. With all the trash talk about your character, your true, unadulterated name has endured slander for thousands of years and your story has survived countless redactions. I think you're a good legend.

What a whirlwind of thoughts and feelings you must've had as you approached the fortress walls of Nineveh, standing high and mighty off the desert floor.

Disrupting

We've got a different kind of murder out here

The man on my TV said

A random kind of feeling starts to fill the air

And we're left here to count the dead

The next channel over

Some ladies were talking

From the Committee of Oh My God

A woman stood up

Started screaming about Satan

The audience roared with applause

And a pollyanna shouted

A pollyanna cried

A pollyanna leapt up

With that sorrow in her eyes

We've got liberty lies and refugees

Big brass bands and amputees

— **Excerpt from** *Liberty Lies* **by David Baerwald and Larry Klein**

Jonah,

You summited the craggy knoll unchaperoned, undefended, and walked into a fortified city governed by jackals. You stood out as you had in Jaffa, though this time it wasn't the sheen from your linens but the brownish sea stains and thread-bareness that immediately drew attention. You looked more like a sea animal than you did a man.

Unbeknownst to you, countless graves laid beneath where you walked, as uninvited strangers were rarely safe in Nineveh. The people's stares made you uncomfortable, leaving you to question, "Will I be hung at noon in the courtyard or pummeled to death by rocks?" The thought of dying now strangely destabilized you. How strange, when just the other day, you requested death so readily!

Common people freely filled the streets, numb to the sickness of their generational ills. Hubris, greed, and misogyny permeated the air. You knew the signs of this sickness, seen in the faces of women shooing their children out of a man's way, and of those same men eyeing any such woman as object and property. But how different was this ugliness from that of your tribe? Or the sailors? Or yourself? If mercy ever resonated with you, Jonah, you knew it required the understanding that darkness lived in all corners, everywhere. Should it be decimated, or mended?

As you stopped to discern your next steps you spotted a great statue of a god you didn't recognize, sculpted from stone. Fighting through the tight crowd, you arrived at its base and hoisted yourself up, with the Lord's message ringing in your ears.

Clearing your throat, you cried out, "People of Nineveh!"

A few turned their heads to listen, but most ignored you.

So, you yelled even louder, "The great and mighty Nineveh will topple in forty days!"

At this, several more gathered, some gripping baskets or carts, others holding animals by the reins. You locked eyes with a stout man in the crowd who reminded you of Amittay. You whispered to yourself, "He would be so proud of me." The crowd appeared slightly alarmed by the proclamation. They eventually wandered off to business as usual, but it seemed a select few were rushing off to spread the word. Taking a deep breath, you moved into a narrow alley and came to rest under a dim lantern.

Within minutes, a young girl approached you, holding a tin of water, smiling. The water tasted so good as it slid down your dry throat. Exquisite kindness glowed from her face. She called out to a young boy, probably her brother, and he appeared at her side. He mumbled something to her that made them both giggle. You surmised they were whispering about how strange you looked. With roles serendipitously reversed, you now were the "other," a nameless riffraff.

After a deep, dreamless night's rest in a barren courtyard, you reappeared in the streets to find everyone in torn shirts and pants, with faces and bare feet covered in black ashes. By the heap of jewels mixed with commoner's clothes, you knew the rich and poor were in repentance together. They looked like a mass of beggars who'd caravanned for months across the desert. But strangely, they all looked relieved, shockingly warm with satisfaction. Apparently, your fiery performance the day before had penetrated their consciousness, motivating them to believe the message of impending doom and, thus, turn to your father's God. Mission accomplished.

A small cohort, known to themselves as the King's Kept, rushed toward you, crying out loudly as they reached to touch your tattered clothes. Your amazement merged with a sadness you couldn't name. In your secret heart, you asked, "Is this a good thing that is happening to these people? . . . If so, am I to surrender to my father's God as well? . . . Was I foolish to have run away? . . . Should I hightail it home? . . . Would they welcome me back or turn me away into exile?" Soon, the people moved on, and you intuited it was time to walk out of this strange city, this bustling metropolis that adopted pious repentance with the speed of a virus.

Making your way toward the front gates, you came upon the king and his entourage standing over a pile of rubble you soon realized had been the stone statue from the day before. The king, wrapped in sackcloth made of goat's hair, leapt to his feet and praised you for condemning idol worship and proclaiming righteous judgement on his people. In the same breath, he took full credit for instituting the city-wide conversion. With bravado, he announced the dire need for his people to practice the laws of the Hebrew God, the very deity who accompanied you now.

"In Nineveh, on the authority of the king and his counselors . . . people and beast alike must appeal to God with fervor . . . all must turn away from the violence they plan against others."[3]

He claimed that submission to this God would secure good fortune, a real win-win for everyone. All of this left you cold on the inside. So, with the gut feeling that this king was at his core a criminal, even now twisting things in his favor, you took your leave.

Looking over your shoulder as you left, you noticed the king smirking among his Kept Men and the sun glint off something near his midriff. They were surreptitiously gloating over a gold filigree waistbelt hidden beneath a thick tuft of sackcloth. Your heart sunk even lower. Right before your eyes was an inflated king, intoxicated with power under the guise of humility. What a deadly cocktail for those in servitude. Did the people need the bidding of an authority to turn from wickedness? Or had a phantom fear gripped them the way it had you, compelling their movements toward Amittay's God? People had died from honest speech before, from doubt and protest. Those graves you walked upon earlier were filled with more than just strangers.

Your effect, a mixture of *true self* dosed with God's stark voice, had animated Nineveh with rarified air, having elevated the fundamental yearning for goodness in the people's consciousness while serendipitously revealing the elements of systemic corruption and control. Sadly, these deathly elements will live on in perpetuity under the guise of the "Believer-King." Best to bet, he will become proficient in religious rhetoric, weaponized with a forked tongue. Your printed story seemingly infers a disturbing truth, living inside our Bibles in the heretical nature of Nineveh's king and the God he had embraced to further his dark reach.

Jonah, you were outside the city gates, beginning the trek back into the wilds, eastward. Your spirit was troubled. Your resolve had been doubly, triply shaken. What does your future hold?

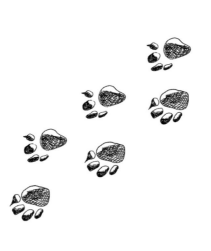

Disintegrating

I guess I lied, you can have everything if there's anything left to have

But I'm pretty picked dry, my bones are all bleached

And my muscles are gone

And my blood's all discolored and oxidized

And my eyes are eaten clean out of my skull

We both fucked up, only I didn't know it then

And you still don't know it now

I didn't know when, and I didn't know how

I should've ran far away where I wouldn't be found

I should've moved across country and lived in the sun

I should've cried on the phone till you knew what you'd done

— **Excerpt from** *Westport to Whidbey* **by Gabriel J. Wheeler**

Jonah,

A fresh set of paw prints at the watering hole where you stopped for a drink triggered the impulse to hurt something. The notion shocked you but felt good to entertain. You nursed it within. And then, without notice or permission, you were ushered into an alternate reality of *knowing*, where you swiftly returned to Nineveh in your mind. There stood the little girl with cup-in-hand and the little boy glued to her side. Dread was all you could feel as you stood staring at their small, beautiful faces.

The little ones simply stood there, wearing even brighter smiles than before. You tried to communicate with them, but they said nothing. You asked yourself the question, "What would have happened to this little girl and boy, along with all the other girls and boys in Nineveh, if their parents *hadn't* heeded your call to repent?" Convinced that they all would've been killed by Amittay's God, you felt ashamed. You thought about hurting yourself, but you didn't want to do God any favors. Apparently, it was His job to kill things.

Among the sun-burnt bushes and brambles on the backside of a lonely hill, you pleaded with the Almighty to throw you down onto the jagged rocks. You whispered, "Take life from me, because for me, death is better than life." When nothing happened, you screamed, "Throw me down upon the rocks like the sailors threw me into the raging sea, I beg of You." For hours, you begged for death, but nothing at all happened. And then, *something* did happen, *something* of the same magnitude as living inside a fish.

Out of thin air, a voice gently asked, "Are you utterly dejected?"[4] It sounded angelic, but how would you know, as you'd never heard an angel speak? Then you remembered a song your mother used to sing at bedtime, the one about the angel who'd been assigned to watch over you. This long-ago memory made you feel so good inside. Next, a blanket of wind gently lifted you high into the air for what felt like an eternity, only to drop you hard on your head.

As your eyes rolled back into focus, you noticed a speck of green sprouting up from the desert floor, rapidly growing into a large plant dressed in luscious green leaves. You nestled under its hefty limbs, which left you feeling sheltered and cared for. You reached toward its stem and thanked it with a hug, breaking into a song of gratitude. As the bond grew, you felt safe enough to ask, "Why are you here and what do you want from me?"

LEAFY PLANT: Jonah, come deeper into the shade I've offered you, to claim what you've needed since leaving your father's house. I'm here to help strengthen you, so you can recover what has been lost. Trust yourself to come further into my covering.

JONAH: I don't know what you mean. Please tell me what I've lost. I'm in no shape to figure that out for myself. I'm feeling so down and out and done. I want something to die, and I'm thinking it's me. Please tell me what I'm fighting against?

LEAFY PLANT: Jonah, you've been running from a deadly enemy, and I am here to provide the covering necessary to face this dreaded foe. Now, trust yourself and come deeper into my shade; simply follow where the energy is directing you.

JONAH: I've gone deeper inside myself and all I can hear are insults condemning me and everything I've done. Whatever this is remains in darkness. I feel powerless to fight back. If I stay here, I'm sure to die. I want to run.

LEAFY PLANT: Stay right where you are, Jonah. You are in the very presence of that which needs to die, and you have the strength inside you to succeed. Stay right where you are, Jonah. Don't run; remain in this place and you will live.

JONAH: I need you to fight this battle for me, as I've never been strong enough to succeed. I'm weak and don't know how to fight. Please release me so I can run away. I beg you to stop this.

You raised your wide eyes and noticed a worm had emerged from a cavity in the desert floor beneath the leafy plant and began to eat away at its succulent stem. The leafy plant cried out in pain as its limbs shriveled and its leaves dried to dust. The worm grew to a gargantuan size as it gluttonously consumed the leafy plant, then immediately shrunk and returned to its hole. With the protective shade now gone, the hot sun returned to its assaultive position in the sky.

Staring into the worm-abyss, you began to cry inwardly for what felt like an eternity. A numen soon appeared to calm your inner chaos and quell the feeling of abandonment that had returned. Now, you were able to clearly comprehend everything that had occurred since walking forlornly out of Nineveh, with special insight into the leafy plant and the death-worm. The green plant was symbolic of your true self, and the murky-colored worm was representative of a predatory spirit, set on taking you down, limb by limb if necessary.

But this also confused you, as the plant died by the worm's violent assault. Did this mean your true self had died or would die in the future? As you began to slip into a depressive state, a light shone from within, revealing more accurately the true nature and meaning of both the plant and the worm.

The *leafy plant* was not your true self but archetypical of your true self. Its function was to leave a deep impression within you, to thrust you into a new understanding of your psychological and spiritual makeup. True self was your essence through and through. Divinity resides inside persons. So, you, Jonah, were divine through and through.

The *death-worm* was not a part of you. It did not live inside you. It existed outside your body. Predatory by nature, this invisible enemy was kept alive by your and the vast collective's choice to remain "unconscious." Being disconnected from true self (and dishonoring a neighbor's true self) keeps the predator alive. Reclamation of your divine strength and giftedness was the only way to stop it.

Armed with the knowledge of both the predator's global scope and personalized attacks, you, Jonah, were relieved from feeling crazy or defective. Walking tall in your body, you arrived back at the watering hole to notice the paw prints now sunbaked. Kneeling down, you gently rested your palms on the crusted prints and suddenly felt that impulse to hurt something drain out of you. From an instinct as old as time, you began to sing a song of freedom and birthright.

Immediately, the air smelled of sweet incense and shimmered golden. The She-Fish's spirit was near.

Empowering

Here's to the babies in a brand new world

Here's to the beauty of the stars

Here's to the travelers on the open road

Here's to the dreamers in the bars

Here's to the teachers in the crowded rooms

Here's to the workers in the fields

Here's to the preachers of the sacred words

Here's to the drivers at the wheel

Here's to you my little loves with blessings from above

Now let the day begin

Here's to you my little loves with blessings from above

Now let the day begin,

Let the day begin

— **Excerpt from** *Let the Day Begin* **by Michael Been**

Jonah,

The jagged rocks you pleaded to be thrown upon, accompanied by the sun-burnt bushes and brambles, now glowed before you as your eyes had become reattuned to beauty. You noticed a different rhythm in your breathing, which felt so pure on the inside. Each step downward felt solid, as if your legs and feet were made from a different material and the ground was surer of itself. As natural as a mountain flower in bloom, you whispered, "I no longer want to die. I want to live." At the base of the lonely hill, you collected stones and wood for the making of an altar, as your heart was grateful.

After half a day's work, you knelt at the foot of the earthen tower and prayed. You noticed when walking away, the surprising height of the altar and a "throne" of sorts at its pinnacle. You were gobsmacked by what you had built with your own hands. A strong impulse to scale the altar and sit on the throne overcame you . . . or nearly did. You stopped as the impulse was clearly a move to inflate, to be full of the wrong kind of power. You said with your interior voice, "I belong with my feet on the ground, where the terebinth, cedar, and cypress trees grow."

The thought of leaving the lonely hill was hard, for a true friendship had been born. You wondered if the hill intuited, as you did, that you would never see one another again. With tears, you thanked the hill for its fellowship, and you *heard* the lonely hill return thanks to you, which left you smiling. Suddenly, you were hit with another impulse, a very different type, a healing and restorative type. Another resurrection. You quickly gathered dry fodder into a clump, rubbed a flame out of thin air, burnt the altar to the ground, and danced with wild abandon through the wafting smoke.

No longer afraid of any strikes from Amittay's God, you returned to the wilderness, flush with integrity and awareness. Your head and heart were perfectly aligned. While kneeling for a sip from the same watering hole as days before, you remembered in detail a past *visionary experience.*

A large mass of people, accompanied by wild and domesticated animals alike, are walking beside an empty basin where cool water once flowed. It's daytime, with the sun burning hot. Leading the crowd are three males dressed in ornate robes, holding lit torches. The people are dressed in shabby work clothes. They've all gone without food and water for days. The men in the crowd have no faces. You intuit a deep pain they collectively carry.

As you look closer, only the women are asking for nourishment, and they are calling for it in song. Their singing becomes louder and louder. The men with no faces begin pleading for permission to walk out of step, to be allowed to disobey orders and go find food and water. They are told by the three robed males to stay in line, to deny their instincts to quell the crowd's hunger and thirst. You feel an undeniable urge to rage against the three robed males but your lips are stitched together with human hair and your hands are fingerless. Suddenly, the three robed males are overcome by a flock of doves, and two of the three are carried off high into the sky. A dark shape swirls around the third robed male left behind. He struggles to breathe as the shape tightens around him, and a blue tear appears in your eye. You know this robed male is an incarnation of God.

You hesitated to recollect more as you knew the danger of inflation, especially the religious type. Also, you were hesitant to encourage the feeling of compassion you had for the lone robed male, as disgust and hatred were all you wanted to feel. Taking several deep breaths, you surrendered to the possibility of more . . .

The robed male motions for you to draw near, even as the dark shape continues to constrict. The threat of danger floods your nerves, but you push yourself toward him. He pleads with you to remove the dark sash swirling around his abdomen, as it is slowly killing him. The jagged knots that make up the dark sash burn your hands as you fight to tear it away. With blood from your palms staining his ornate robe, he begins to swoon back and forth, wailing louder and louder.

Suddenly, the dark sash breaks into tiny threads and is replaced by a second sash that dazzles with every color in the universe. The robed figure asks you to remove the colorful sash from his waist and tie it around your own. Touching the colorful sash immediately heals your bloody palms, and you're astonished to see it's made from fresh fish gills. With the healing sash secured around your waist, the figure, now appearing as a desert priest, asks for your permission to return to Nineveh and care for the prisoners of the demented king. You stand dumbfounded but utter, "Yes." Suddenly, the priest morphs into a beautiful stag and leaps off into the wilderness. As he fades from view, the large mass of people reappears, accompanied by their animals. Their children are carrying baskets of every fruit while the river gushes with clean water.

You came back to yourself by the watering hole and sat cross-legged on its bank. As if from a lightning bolt, you were struck by a childish panic, sparking a memory from long ago.

In the early morning of the seventh day of the tenth month of your twelfth year, you had gone to fetch water for the family breakfast, like you did every morning. But this time, you returned with a dry bucket. When your mother asked, "Why no water?" you had no recollection of even being at the river, though your sandals were caked with mud.

Then it hit you! The vision of the people and the animals and the robed men and the sashes . . . it had come to you at the river's edge at the ripe age of twelve. You'd bottled it up and hidden it away, as it was too much for a boy to hold. Now, as a differentiated adult, you were strong enough to embrace the vision and extract meaning from its rich and mystical content.

Memories of rituals performed in your village prompted you to gather artifacts from the desert floor. With your hands wet from the watering hole, you patted mud into squares to construct a circular barrier. Holding an olive branch obviously scarred by lightning, you imagined burning images into the golden sand. Flames appeared in your mind, igniting the branch's tip, and you began wielding it in the air like a warrior's sword or a prophet's staff. Your imagination was ablaze!

Carving a snake-like trench symbolized the eternal river now flowing with fresh cool water. The stones you placed along its banks represented thousands upon thousands of people freely sharing the earth's bounty. You plastered the area with "baskets of fresh fruit." You imagined men from all walks of life surrendering their anger and hurt, to find peace inside themselves. You drew images of flowers, depicting women coming into their own strength and fortitude to restore peace among their people, as they held the keys to wisdom and beauty.

You stacked dead debris from the desert floor into misshapen piles and imagined them to be robes worn by doomsmen. You imagined these tall piles catching fire, soon rendering a dark ash covering the desert floor as far as the eyes could see. You intuited a new spirit being unleashed into the world. You honored the sacrifice by heaving dried leaves into the air while singing at the top of your lungs a song of liberation. Falling backward onto the golden sand, you stared into the wide sky above with the eyes of a young dove. Now quietly humming, a memory flashed of your father drinking from a chalice and singing the very song you'd just sung.

At the mouth of the eternal river, you sketched with your bare hands the face of a beautiful fish. You gently pressed your fingers onto your lips as if to unstitch them and announced, "Amittay's God has been overthrown!" You felt zero fear as you continued to speak this truth; with gratitude, you blew a kiss to the She-Fish. With imagination at high altitude, you interpreted your artwork as a *coherent whole made of distinctive parts*. You saw yourself and the world as *whole*. You prayed your masterpiece would endure the harsh desert environment for the next exile to find his or her way. Kneeling, you thanked the watering hole for the gifts she had given.

After a long day's walk, you stopped to enjoy a meal of tubers and nuts and again stared into the wide sky above; this time, it was full of moonlight and stars. You fell fast asleep and dreamed about *anima* and *animus*, the feminine and masculine spheres of the soul, respectively. The dream was *prophetic*, its characteristics being a *foretaste*, as the evolutionary process would impart the meaning of *anima* and *animus* into consciousness at a future time in history. For in your lifetime, the soul would remain bereft of such specific language.

You awoke the next morning, feeling inspired and hopeful about the future. You thought hard about the night's dream. One question hovered in your mind like a moth drawn to a flame, "Were you still a prophet?" You felt amazingly light rather than heavy from the question. Then, you remembered three events from the past and understood the night's dream had returned them to your memory, all three having been altered in their outcomes.

You fell asleep in the hull of that ship headed for Joppa. The sailor woke you, asking who you were and where you came from. He invited you upstairs where you joined others for a meal of fresh fish and vegetables and a pint. When a violent storm arose, neither you nor God were blamed for it. All on board survived and gave thanks.

Your mother is within the center of the brightest light. She held the young lamb traumatized by that pack of young boys. She motioned for them to come close, and they encircled your mother holding the terrorized lamb. The males cried and asked how to make amends for their violence. Your mother said, "You already have, now go in peace."

You're sitting with Ahmose on the bank of the slow river. Her smile glowed like the moon. You talked for hours. As the night fire went out, you fell asleep in each other's arms. When the day broke, you lit the fire to brew some morning tea. Returning home, you two shared a meal with both sets of parents and joyfully discussed your wedding plans.

Possibly, the night's dream had answered the question, "Were you still a prophet?" Because without you, Jonah, these beautiful outcomes regarding sailors, mothers, and lovers wouldn't have happened. Could it be that true "prophesy" is nothing more than yearning for the best for all people and committing one's life to overcoming hate with love?

Concerning the dream's three events, the ship for Joppa had long since sailed, and your dear mother would have likely made peace with the young upstarts. But what of Ahmose and the wedding attended by joyful parents? "I will go find her," you promised yourself.

As you began walking westward, you trusted the road would lead you home. Your mind gently turned toward your father, and the hope flowered that he'd receive you as his beloved son. In your long shadow before you, God's face appeared again. Or was that the shape of a fish?

Conclusion

Like Jonah, we are wise to ask what direction we are heading. Are we living our own authentic life or are we living a life prescribed to us from many influences?

In *Inner Work: Using Dreams and Active Imagination for Personal Growth*, Jungian analyst Robert A. Johnson aptly says, "A great sense of security develops from this process of individuation. One begins to understand that it isn't necessary to struggle to be like someone else, for by being one's own self one stands on the surest ground."[5]

You've traveled alongside Jonah on his harrowing journey toward selfhood. Imagine each chapter of the book as a station of transformation, a piece of landscape where Jonah truly *lived* his unfolding life. While holding images of Jonah's journey in your mind, move your focus to your own journey. Allow your thoughts to be what they are, without altering them according to what they're supposed to be and allow yourself to feel what you feel.

What follows are the nine-chapter headings uniquely formatted for thoughtful action:

Ruminating

Honor the thoughts and feelings you're having about getting free from something or someone that is holding you back. Pour your psychological energy toward the issue and trust your ability to remain steadfast.

What person, place or thing has become oppressive to you?

Do you have the inner capacity necessary to get freer?

With your head and heart aligned, go within and *locate your longing for authenticity.*

Running

It's time to leave the abusive relationship, the toxic workplace, the political and/or religious tribe that restricts you and no longer represents the person you're becoming. You've outgrown whatever or whomever is keeping you down.

What action-step is required for you to break away?

Can you locate the inner confidence necessary to follow through?

With your head and heart aligned, go within and *locate your longing to leave.*

Sinking

You've been mistreated with no genuine invitation to be understood. Or perhaps you've made a grave mistake (or series of mistakes), resulting in painful consequences. You feel rejected by others (and yourself) and deserving of being "thrown overboard."

What part of your inner life is crying out to be acknowledged?

Can you turn toward this part of you to graciously befriend it?

With your head and heart aligned, go within and *locate your longing to know yourself.*

Settling

You have hurts and disappointments that need to feel the clean, clear light of acceptance. So often, we need someone to show us what this acceptance looks like or sounds like before we can offer it to ourselves.

Are you able to imagine an advocate rescuing a part of you?

Do you find it possible to hear this inner advocate address you?

With your head and heart aligned, go within and *locate your longing for true acceptance.*

Rising

Life is difficult, sometimes overwhelming. To rise to our feet takes an inner strength that often seems out of reach. New growth is directly correlated to the discovery of a new part of our personality, a part hidden in the unconscious.

Are you trusting enough to allow a new energy to rise inside you?

Is there enough self-permission to move forward into the unknown?

With your head and heart aligned, go within and *locate your longing for new strength.*

Differentiating

Gaining freedom to walk an unknown path in life can make all the difference in the world. Sometimes, a decision must be made that proves difficult to live out and difficult (or impossible) for another to honor and accept.

Is your mind clear enough to imagine a separation from a false form of you?

Will the personal world you live in accept a truer form of you?

With your head and heart aligned, go within and *locate your longing to be released (or rereleased).*

Disrupting

"Leaders" whose narcissistic motives are veiled behind a false front of concern for the common good are in endless supply. The willingness for the marginalized to confront these individuals and the organizations they govern takes courage.

What will it require from you to protest an injustice in your midst?

What part of you will vigilantly oppose confronting this injustice?

With your head and heart aligned, go within and *locate your longing for justice.*

Disintegrating

We are easily seduced into abandoning our power and left vulnerable to the whims of something other than ourselves. All forms of ruling authorities can take up residence within us. This causes great distress in our mind, body, and spirit.

Can you turn toward that lone wilderness that resides deep inside you?

Are you able to invite a lost part to come forth from this wilderness?

With your head and heart aligned, go within and *locate your longing for inner authority.*

Empowering

We are born with the capability to empower ourselves psychologically, emotionally, and spiritually. This takes dedication and patience due to the trauma we've experienced; we can all attest that life is destabilizing.

Are you able to voice your birth name without perpetual apology?

How do you envision being truer in the life unfolding before you?

With your head and heart aligned, go within and *locate your longing for wholeness.*

Old Testament theologian Walter Brueggemann identifies two barriers to communion with God in his groundbreaking book *Finally Comes the Poet*: "an *exaggerated self* that gives God no access; or there is an *exaggerated God* who permits nothing of us in the transaction."[6] Regarding the latter, Brueggemann petitions for "speech of crushed human voices, persons too long engaged in denial, too long burdened with superfluous guilt, too long pent-up with rage, speech that must burst open in impolite ways in order to rush against an overstated God."[7]

To see Jonah overruled by an *exaggerated God* is to call upon the Christian church to stop reducing him into a cowardly dissenter; recasting Jonah as one committed to divine fidelity and autonomy of self resurrects his dignity and worth. The freed Jonah carries the voice of a buoyant hope, beginning at the level of the *personal* and coalescing into the realm of the *universal*. This voice is articulated by freed speech that authorizes and energizes better selves ultimately for a much better world.

We owe Jonah a debt of gratitude for showing us what messy authenticity looks like, what embracing self *feels* like. And we owe ourselves for enduring (and sometimes overcoming) the hardships that attend being consciously human. The trinity of SELF (core being), CITY (human ecosystem), and GOD (divine presence) cannot become stale or be held hostage. It must be revived in every age and *reimagined* in every light.

Works Cited

*J. Philip Newell, *Celtic Benediction: Morning and Night Prayer* (Grand Rapids: Wm. B. Eerdmans Publishing Co., 2000), 22.

1. Jack M. Sasson, *Jonah: A New Translation with Introduction, Commentary, and Interpretation* (New York: Doubleday / Bantam Doubleday Dell Publishing Group, Inc., 1990), 3.

2. Sasson, *Jonah*, 5.

3. Sasson, *Jonah*, 5.

4. Sasson, *Jonah*, 5.

5. Robert A. Johnson, *Inner Work: Using Dreams and Active Imagination for Personal Growth* (New York: HarperOne, 1989), 12.

6. Walter Brueggemann, *Finally Comes The Poet* (Minneapolis: Augsburg Fortress, 1989), 49.

7. Brueggemann, *Finally Comes The Poet*, 50.

Song Credits

Tip of My Tongue
Words and Music by Mark Heard
Copyright © 1992 Ideola Music
All Rights Administered by BMG Rights Management (US) LLC
All Rights Reserved. Used by Permission.
Reprinted by Permission of Hal Leonard LLC

Flown This Acid World
Words and Music by Peter Himmelman
Copyright © 1992 HIMMASONGS and UNIVERSAL-GEFFEN MUSIC
All Rights Administered by UNIVERSAL-GEFFEN MUSIC
All Rights Reserved. Used by Permission.
Reprinted by Permission of Hal Leonard LLC

Behind Blue Eyes
Words and Music by Peter Townshend
Copyright © 1971 Fabulous Music Ltd.
Copyright Renewed
All Rights Administered in the USA and Canada by Spirit
Four Music, Suolubaf Music and ABKCO Music Inc.
International Copyright Secured. All Rights Reserved.
Reprinted by Permission of Hal Leonard LLC

Lost
Words and Music by Sienna Meadow
All Rights Reserved. Reprinted by Permission of Sienna Meadow

Acknowledgements

The fierce soul and deep intellect of my life partner, Lori, who is also a writer, kept me tethered to re-telling Jonah's painful story. My son Gabriel's skill in rich storytelling and composition freed my writer's block midway through the project. My son Caleb's expertise in creative production, along with his keen filmmaker's eye, helped to shape this book and carry it to the finish line. Their partners, Lauren and Ashley, respectively, offered rich input which shaped my writing. These five empowered me in ways which are beyond words.

The Rev. Dr. Jerry Smith, S.T.D., helped me to discover my inner Jonah and save me when I was drowning.

Walter Brueggemann has mentored me with friendship and with an academic rigor that has ignited my mind in reimagining scripture.

Peter Michael Boyd, my loving friend, kindly and earnestly listened to my earliest iterations of Jonah. He is gone from this world, but never forgotten.

Saint Mark's Episcopal Cathedral in Seattle hosted my presentation of the earliest formations of this book, and I appreciate those who attended for offering feedback and encouragement.

To all the other good people who supported me these last six years, I thank you.

On The Author

Doug Wheeler, DPhil, is a licensed psychotherapist of 35 years.

He works at the intersection of psychology and spiritual formation, integrating head and heart for the actualization of the true Self.

Reimagining Jonah: *A Flight to Freedom* is his debut book.